Warts & All

I dedicate *Warts and All* **to Martina, Siofra, Sean and Brenainn –** *my heart and soul*

First published in 2008 by
Appletree Press Ltd
The Old Potato Station
14 Howard Street South
Belfast BT7 1AP

Tel: + 44 (0) 28 90 24 30 74
Fax: + 44 (0) 28 90 24 67 56
Web site: www.appletree.ie
Email: reception@appletree.ie

A catalogue record for this book is available from the British Library.

Warts and All – Ten Years of the Good Friday Agreement

ISBN-13: 978 1 84758 105 1

Desk and Marketing Editor: Jean Brown
Copy-Editor: Jim Black
Designer: Annette Nugent
Production Manager: Paul McAvoy

9 8 7 6 5 4 3 2 1

AP3579

Warts & All

Ten Years of the Good Friday Agreement

John Kennedy

Appletree Press

About the Author:

Born in County Tyrone, John Kennedy graduated from the University of Ulster, Belfast in 1990 with a BA Honours Degree in Design. For others, the next step was to seek full-time employment in that field but John chose the precarious route of becoming a freelance cartoonist. For years it was a daunting task but his dogged determination finally paid off in 1998 after the signing of the Good Friday Agreement when he combined his unique style with politics. Various newspapers and magazines throughout Ireland and the United States have published his illustrations and his yearly exhibitions have been well received.

For more information and examples of his work, visit his homepage on:

http://kennedycartoons.com

Foreword by Sam Millar

It is an honour for me to be asked to write the foreword to John Kennedy's *Warts and All*. In a book full of visually arresting images and astonishingly varied subjects, Kennedy has given us a subtle yet sometimes brutal vignette of miscreants, duplicitous politicians, and the occasional clown without the make-up.

Like all genuine artists, his work is neither neutral nor ambiguous, and his intolerance of social injustice and political buffoonery is clearly highlighted in the compositions held within this book. Each illustration will make you laugh, may even make you cry, some may even make you angry. If so, he has done what he set out to do: create a memorable and timely book of classic satire and caricatures exposing the warts and all of society and its inhabitants in sharply acerbic, uncompromising drawings.

No politician escapes his methodical, almost surgical eye – and rightly so. His ammunition is his ink, and may the gods help any politician in the line of fire from that ink. Fiercely independent, this fighting spirit has rewarded him, over the years, the ultimate honour bestowed upon any artist worth their salt: censorship. Despite the narrow-mindedness of the censors, Kennedy has been widely published in the USA and Europe, with his work appearing in *The Irish Herald, The Irish Gazette, Irish Sunday Mirror, The Blanket, Londonderry Sentinel, Sunday Journal, Daily Ireland, Citizen Magazine, Fortnight Magazine,* and *Channel* 4, to name but a few of a quickly expanding list.

Finally, if a picture truly paints a thousand words, then Kennedy has given us enough words to fill a library. Make this compelling and brilliantly constructed book part of **your** library. It has classic written – and *drawn* – all over it…

Sam Millar, best-selling author, *On The Brinks*

10 April 1998 (Good Friday)
After two years of intensive negotiations, the Northern
Ireland peace process reached a climax when multi-party
talks at Stormont produced a 65-page document that
would draw a line under almost 30 years of violence.

Reaction to the Agreement from people and organisations
around the world was very positive, but the big test for
the British and Irish governments was to persuade the
local electorate that this was the only way forward.

22 May 1998 In separate referendums, people from both sides of the border vote overwhelmingly in favour of The Good Friday Agreement.

24 May 1998 Anti-agreement politicians claim they secured a majority 'No Vote' within Unionism and vow to oppose any power-sharing government.

15 August 1998 A Real IRA car bomb kills 29 people and injures 220 in Omagh, Co. Tyrone.

3 September 1998 During his second visit to the North, US President Bill Clinton urges everyone to focus on the peace process, no matter what happens.

29 March 1999 The Provisional IRA claim responsibility for the abduction, murder and disappearance of nine people between 1972 and 1981.

4 July 1999 For the first time in five years, the Drumcree dispute passes off relatively peacefully.

3 August 1999 The first Community Restorative Justice office opens in nationalist West Belfast.

9 September 1999 Chris Patten's radical report into policing gets a frosty reception from Unionists, describing it as 'a shoddy piece of work'.

11 February 2000   Secretary of State Peter Mandelson (October 1999–January 2001) pulls the plug on the new power-sharing Executive after the Independent International Commission on Decommissioning (IICD) "received no information from the PIRA as to when decommissioning will start".

27 March 2000 A public hearing into the events of Bloody Sunday begins at the Guildhall, Derry.

31 May 2001 Secretary of State John Reid (January 2001–October 2002) claims that the new plastic bullets issued to the Security Forces were "on balance a great deal safer that the existing ones".

23 October 2001 After months of stalemate, the Independent International Commission on Decommissioning (IICD) announce that the PIRA have begun the process of decommissioning their weapons.

17 March 2002 Top-secret paramilitary documents are stolen from one of Northern Ireland's most secure bases.

14 October 2002 The British Government suspend devolution after Sinn Fein offices at Stormont are raided over alleged intelligence gathering.

24 February 2003 The Assets Recovery Agency, headed by former Assistant Chief Constable Alan McQuillan, begin targeting paramilitaries involved in organised crime.

29 March 2003 Gerry Adams announces that he can foresee a situation where his party would support policing.

27 November 2003   Northern Ireland politics become more extreme when DUP and Sinn Fein emerge as the two largest parties in the second Assembly elections.

29 November 2003 While Sinn Fein pushed for the Assembly to be reinstated, the DUP insisted that a new deal had to be sought first.

3 February 2004 An upsurge in paramilitary activity forces the British and Irish Governments to review the Good Friday Agreement at Stormont.

28 March 2004 Ulster Unionist David Trimble survives an internal leadership challenge from Coleraine-based management consultant David Hoey.

4 April 2004 Retired Canadian Judge, Peter Cory finds evidence of state involvement in four high profile murders: Robert Hamill, LVF leader Billy Wright, solicitors Pat Finucane and Rosemary Nelson.

25 April 2004 The Independent Monitoring Commission's (IMC) first report recommends financial sanctions against Sinn Fein and the Progressive Unionist Party, in response to continuing PIRA and UVF violence.

11 July 2004 According to media reports, Pope John Paul II may include the North in his next Ireland visit.

25 July 2004 Sinn Fein's Conor Murphy voices his concerns that demilitarization is not happening quickly enough.

5 December 2004 The prospect of any deal before Christmas hangs in the balance.

30 January 2005 Tempers flare at Government Buildings, Dublin, between Gerry Adams and Taoiseach Bertie Ahern over the Northern Bank raid.

4 February 2005 Accusations of Provisional IRA criminality prompts 'P. O'Neill' to release a statement accusing the British and Irish Governments of wilfully pandering to Securocrat mischief.

6 February 2005 The DUP's Justice spokesman Ian Paisley Jnr describes the marriage of UUP adviser Dr Steven King as "immoral, offensive and obnoxious".

4 March 2005 The PSNI announces that it has purchased 50,000 Attenuated Energy Projectiles (New Plastic Bullets) for the upcoming Marching Season.

4 March 2005 Leader Gerry Adams addresses the Sinn Fein Ard Fheis, Dublin.

5 March 2005 Gerry Kelly informs the party faithful that policing structures would throw up serious challenges for Republicans.

17 March 2005 The murder of Robert McCartney by the Provisional IRA in January dominates the political debate in Washington during St Patrick's Day celebrations.

3 April 2005 Sinn Fein's General Secretary, Mitchel McLaughlin and new SDLP leader Mark Durkan debate who is best to succeed John Hume as Foyle MP.

24 April 2005 Sitting MP Pat Doherty and SDLP Assembly Member Eugene McMenamin refuse hospital campaigner Dr Kieran Deeny a free run in West Tyrone.

6 May 2005 Ulster Unionist leader David Trimble loses his Upper Bann Westminster seat to the DUP.

24 June 2005   East Belfast Assembly Member Reg Empey is elected new leader of the Ulster Unionist Party.

10 July 2005 The Orange Order refuse to hold face-to-face talks with the Bogside Residents Group to defuse tensions in Derry over the Twelfth.

28 July 2005 The Provisional IRA formally orders an end to its armed campaign.

5 August 2005 Having successfully smuggled the Colombia Three back into the Irish Republic, the Provos plan their next move.

12 October 2005 At a public meeting in South Belfast, Father Alec Reid compares the Unionist community to Nazis.

16 December 2005 After his release from jail over the Stormontgate affair, Sinn Fein's head of administration, Denis Donaldson confirms to the media that he was a British spy for 20 years.

24 January 2006 During a meeting in Downing Street, Ian Paisley tells Tony Blair that Republican racketeering will not be tolerated.

8 February 2006 Sinn Fein's Westminster allowances are withdrawn after the Northern Bank robbery.

17 March 2006 For the second year running Sinn Fein are prevented by the Bush administration to fund-raise in the USA.

20 April 2006 Secretary of State Peter Hain declares that 24th November deadline to restore devolution is 'immovable'.

15 May 2006 A political row breaks out when PUP leader David Ervine establishes an alliance with the UUP during a recalled Assembly meeting.

30 May 2006 Sinn Fein's chief negotiator Martin McGuinness dismisses claims from the DUP and a Sunday tabloid that he is an MI6 agent.

30 June 2006 Social Development Minister David Hanson announces that the British Government is to spend £104,000 to help develop the Twelfth of July as a major tourism event.

3 August 2006 A bloody UDA feud is averted after some of its members are ousted from North Belfast.

12 August 2006   Despite strong opposition from the main governing body of the GAA, Sinn Fein hold a rally to commemorate the 25th anniversary of the 1981 Hunger Strike in Casement Park, Belfast.

27 September 2006 Taoiseach Bertie Ahern comes under severe pressure to resign after it is revealed that he received payments from wealthy businessmen while he was Finance Minister in 1993.

26 October 2006 Bloody Sunday chairman Lord Saville informs the victims' families that his report would not be ready until early 2008.

24 November 2006 Attempts to restore devolution are interrupted when Loyalist killer Michael Stone is apprehended entering Stormont with guns and explosives.

29 December 2006 Ian Paisley suggests that power-sharing may be possible, if Sinn Fein were to endorse policing.

9 January 2007 Sinn Fein and the SDLP raise concerns about the new MI5 headquarters being built in Holywood, Co. Down.

13 January 2007 At a special meeting in Dublin, senior members of Sinn Fein give Gerry Adams the necessary two-thirds vote to hold an Ard Fheis on policing at the end of the month.

22 January 2007 Police Ombudsman Nuala O'Loan publishes evidence that RUC Special Branch and a UVF gang from North Belfast colluded in 16 murders.

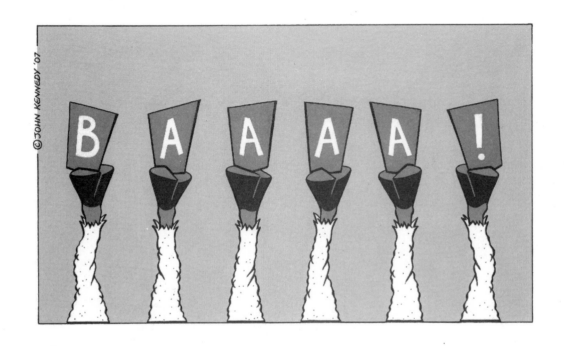

28 January 2007   At an extraordinary Ard Fheis in the RDS, Dublin, Sinn Fein passes a motion to support the PSNI and the criminal justice system in the North.

7 February 2007 Policing Board Chairman Desmond Rea hits out at Mark Durkan's claim that the SDLP influenced the decision to appoint Hugh Orde as Chief Constable, instead of policemen from the "old RUC order".

20 February 2007   The British Government announce that they will provide £130 million to help build a new policing college in Cookstown, Co. Tyrone.

8 March 2007 Nuala O'Loan confirms that she is investigating six incidents of collusion between the Provisional IRA and British Security Forces.

22 March 2007 The British Government give the UDA £1.2 million to help them transform into a non-paramilitary group.

26 March 2007   In front of an astonished audience, Ian Paisley and Gerry Adams sit side by side for their first news conference in Stormont, and announce that power-sharing may be possible by 8th May.

10 April 2007 Breandan MacCionnaith resigns from Sinn Fein over speculation that a deal was done with the DUP to allow an Orange parade down the Garvaghy Road.

3 May 2007 The Ulster Volunteer Force declares that it has renounced violence and criminality, but will retain their weaponry.

8 May 2007 First Minister Ian Paisley and his deputy Martin McGuinness take their pledge of office and devolution is returned to Northern Ireland after five years of direct rule.

15 May 2007 Sinn Fein president Gerry Adams is forced to condemn the murder of Detective Garda Jerry McCabe, gunned down in Adare, Co. Limerick by a PIRA gang during a botched Post Office robbery in 1996.

26 May 2007   Sinn Fein's ambitions to be in government, north and south of the border, are dashed with a very poor performance in the Republic's General Election.

22 June 2007 The British Government announce that the new Independent Consultative Group co-chaired by Denis Bradley and former Archbishop of Armagh, Robin Eames is the best way to deal with the legacy of the Troubles.

26 June 2007 Despite suggesting we should draw a line under the past as PSNI Oversight Commissioner, former Canadian Mountie Al Hutchinson is appointed to succeed Nuala O'Loan as Police Ombudsman.

4 July 2007 Sports Minister Edwin Poots comes under pressure from within the DUP over his support for a multi-sports stadium at the former Maze prison site.

31 July 2007   After 38 years of Operation Banner, the British Army reduce their presence in Northern Ireland to a garrison of 5000 – Operation Helvetic.

12 August 2007 During a Republican rally in Belfast, Gerry Adams calls on the British Government to "acknowledge the truth" about collusion.

3 September 2007 Senior Northern Ireland politicians, including Deputy First Minister Martin McGuinness, attend talks in Finland in an attempt to end sectarian violence in Iraq.

5 October 2007 The UDA issues a statement indicating that it will not be pressurized into decommissioning.

16 October 2007 In the absence of UDA decommissioning, Social Development Minister Margaret Ritchie stands alone and withdraws the £1.2 million of government funding allocated to Loyalist projects.

8 November 2007 Republican commitment to the peace process is questioned after two murders by the Provos and an attempted murder of a PSNI officer by the Real IRA.

11 November 2007 At a Remembrance Sunday commemoration, UDA Brigadier Jackie McDonald announces that the Ulster Freedom Fighters has been stood down.

29 November 2007 Sinn Fein Councillor Tom Hartley (middle) chairs the first District Policing Partnership (DPP) meeting in West Belfast.

7 December 2007 MEP Jim Allister officially launches the Traditional Unionist Voice, a new political movement that will oppose the power-sharing Executive.

7 December 2007 Northern Ireland's First and Deputy First Minister meet President George W. Bush during an investment drive in the US.

31 January 2008 Caitriona Ruane walks out of a committee meeting after Sammy Wilson criticises her performance as Education Minister.

4 March 2008 After months of speculation, Ian Paisley announces he will stand down as First Minister.

8 April 2008 The families of victims killed in the Omagh bomb launch a lawsuit against the five alleged leaders of the Real IRA in Belfast's High Court.

7 May 2008 More than 100 corporate executives from America arrive in Northern Ireland for a three-day investment conference.

22 May 2008 The British Government calls on Loyalist paramilitaries to cooperate with the Independent International Commission on Decommissioning (IICD) before it dissolves in 2010.

29 May 2008 The Consultative Group on the Past co-chaired by Lord Eames and Denis Bradley outline ways in which the State could acknowledge their full and complex role in the Troubles.

5 June 2008 New Democratic Unionist Party (DUP) leader Peter Robinson is appointed First Minister to the Northern Ireland Assembly.

16 June 2008 US President George W. Bush meets new First Minister Peter Robinson and Deputy First Minister Martin McGuinness during his fleeting visit to Northern Ireland.

Other books by Appletree Press:

John Pepper's Complete Norn Iron Haunbook
John Pepper

The people of Ulster have, over the years moulded the English language into something distinctively, and some would say quite uniquely, their own. *John Pepper's Complete Norn Iron Haunbook* is a hilarious and indispensible guide for anyone wishing to master the morr tung of *Norn Iron* or who simply needs advice on blending in with the locals.

'I don't advise reading John Pepper among a crowd of strangers or they'll probably think you're daft when you do as I did and start laughing aloud.'
Ulster Star

ISBN-13: 978 0 86281 913 2

The Bumper Irish Jokebook
Terry Adlam

The Bumper Irish Jokebook is just what you need for a taste of Irish humour. Here's a taster from over 800 jokes to whet your appetite for a feast of fun!

An Irishwoman went to see her doctor. 'It's my son, Doctor,' she said. ' He keeps making mud pies and eating them.'
'Nothing to worry about,' said the Doctor. 'He'll grow out of it.'
'I hope so, Doctor. His wife is getting very upset.'

ISBN-13: 978 1 84785 045 0

The World's Best Hangover Cures
Alex Benady

The World's Best Hangover Cures has just what every occasional or regular tippler is looking for – advice on that great leveller of mankind, the hangover!
No matter how great or lowly your stature in life the hangover is the one thing that drinkers of all races, creeds and indeed nationalities suffer in common. So here are details of how our ancestors and friends from overseas have coped with the 'sorrow at the end of drunkenness'! Funky urban-style drawings ensure that even if your own hangover cures aren't making the spinning room or your spinning stomach settle you will at least be able to raise a smile at the antics of those who are even worse off than you.
Cheers!

ISBN-13: 978 0 86281 990 3